ABC Halloween Witch

ABC
Halloween
Witch

By Ida DeLage

Drawings by Lou Cunette

GARRARD PUBLISHING COMPANY
CHAMPAIGN, ILLINOIS

ABC Halloween Witch

This is a witch.
She is the ABC witch.

A AWAY

The ABC witch
flies **AWAY**.
She flies **AWAY**
into the sky.

B BROOM

The ABC witch
flies on her **BROOM**.

C CAVE

The witch flies
to her **CAVE**.

D DARK

Her cave is **DARK**.

It is **DARK, DARK, DARK!**

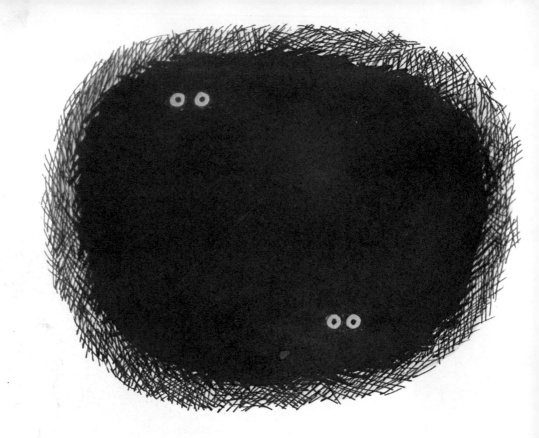

E EYES

The ABC witch
has big, green **EYES**.
Her green **EYES** can see
in the dark, dark cave.

F FIRE

The ABC witch
makes a **FIRE**.

G GLOWS

The fire **GLOWS**

in the dark cave.

H HEAVY

The big pumpkin
is **HEAVY**.

I IDEA

The ABC witch has
an **IDEA**!

J JACK-O'-LANTERN

She makes an ABC
JACK-O'-LANTERN.

K KIDS

The ABC witch
scares the little **KIDS**
with the jack-o'-lantern.

L LAUGHS

The witch **LAUGHS**.

"Hee-hee-hee!"

She **LAUGHS** and **LAUGHS**.

17

M MASKS

The little kids
have **MASKS**.
Now they will scare
the ABC witch.

N NOTHING

But **NOTHING** scares
the ABC witch.
She still laughs.
"Hee-hee-hee!"

O OLD

The ABC witch is **OLD**.
Her cat is **OLD**.

P POT

The witch has
a big **POT**.

Q QUEER

The witch puts
some **QUEER** things
into her pot.

R RATS

RATS run all over
the cave.

S SPELL

The ABC witch
makes a magic **SPELL**.

T TOAD

She puts a spell
on a **TOAD**.

U UNICORN

Oh oh!
Now the toad
is a **UNICORN**.
What a magic spell!

V VANISH!

The witch says,
"**VANISH!**"
The unicorn is gone.

W WIND

The **WIND** blows.

Whoo-oo-oo.

X SIX

SIX more witches
come.

Y YELL

They **YELL**
"Eee-ee-ee!"

Z ZOOM

All of the witches
ZOOM off
into the dark night.
It is HALLOWEEN!